The Ultimate
EXECUTIVE LUNCH

by Professor Tymus Munney
The ultimate executive manual
to titillate the mind and the palate

HURLEY STYLE

THE ULTIMATE EXECUTIVE LUNCH FEATURES:

* No calories

* No cholesterol

* No triglycerides

* No salt

* No vitamins

* No carbohydrates

* No starch

* No indigestion

* No food

"In our opinion
food should be sniffed lustily at table,
both as a precaution and as a matter of enjoyment,
the sniffing of it to be regarded
in the same light as the tasting of it."

E. B. WHITE
Every Day Is Saturday

INTRODUCTION

All good ideas are simple and this one is about as simple as you can get.

You want to eat less and lose weight?
You want to save time at the office?
You want to save money on expensive lunches?
You want to learn more about business?
This book achieves it all for you.

Here's how:

There are five basic senses:
Touch
Smell
Taste
Sight
Hearing

The act of eating involves all of these but mostly taste, sight and smell. Professor Tymus Munney has developed THE ULTIMATE EXECUTIVE LUNCH by simply removing two out of these three.
Good presentation of food is preferable to a sloppy mess on the plate but is largely to blame for the rise of the cult of Nouvelle Cuisine – skimpy, pathetic little portions but very artistically arranged on the plate. Sight plays no part in THE ULTIMATE EXECUTIVE LUNCH.
The removal of the taste sensations cleverly avoids the act of swallowing – so no ingestion of calories, cholesterol, salt, triglycerides and the many other components of food which, in one way or another, experts tell you are harmful.
You are left with the OLEFACTORY sensations of food – the mouth watering fragrances that assail the nostrils and stimulate the anticipation of the pleasures to come. The master stroke of THE ULTIMATE EXECUTIVE LUNCH is that it stops right there. No chewing, no swallowing, no wondering if it's good for you. Simply a menu each day to titillate and satisfy your sense of smell. No timewasting at the restaurant or staff dining room. No hassle with who pays the bill. No time away from the important task of making money. Just sit at your desk and scratch the labels for each day's Menu.

Because man cannot live by bread alone each day's Menu is accompanied by worthwhile thoughts on the subject of business and its related activities. As you enjoy your lunch – read, mark, learn and inwardly digest these morsels of wit and wisdom – if you stick by the book it's the only sustenance you are going to get for lunch.
If you need sustenance in more solid form – for instance actual food, don't take this book seriously. You can still enjoy it with a hamburger, salad, pizza, Beluga caviare, or whatever your pleasure. If you are serious about dieting, there are plenty of authoritative books to advise you but this is not one of them.
THE ULTIMATE EXECUTIVE LUNCH does offer one real dieting possibility – best stated by E. V. Knox in his book "Gorgeous Times".

"Five muffins are enough for any man at any one meal, and the breast and wing of a chicken should suffice without attacking the fibrous legs. Very different, however, is the case of pâté de fois gras, sandwiches, oysters and meringues. I cannot eat too many of these. I make it, therefore, my rule to consume very limited quantities of plain food in order to leave as much room as possible for delicacies."

By following this simple philosophy and using this book for lunch you could limit your eating of plain lunch-time food to leave room for gastronomic treats which are more likely to be available in the evening from your own kitchen or at a relaxing dining venue at the end of your hard day's toil.

Enjoy your lunches and remember
You are learning
You are slimming
You are saving time
You are saving money

What more can you expect from lunch?

When a man tells you that he got rich through hard work,
ask him whose?
DONALD ROBERT PERRY MARQUIS

All generalizations are dangerous,
even this one.
ALEXANDER DUMAS

Name the greatest of all inventors. Accident.
MARK TWAIN

Select stocks the way porcupines make love —
very carefully.
ROBERT DINDA

Conscience is, in most men,
an anticipation of the opinion of others.
SIR HENRY TAYLOR

A politician is one who thinks twice
before saying nothing.
ANON

A little learning is a dangerous thing,
but none at all is fatal.
VISCOUNT SAMUEL

It is better to know nothing
than to know what ain't so.
JOSH BILLINGS

Money, it turned out, was exactly like Sex.
You thought of nothing else if you didn't have it,
and thought of other things if you did.
JAMES A. BALDWIN

The percentage of error will multiply
the longer you deliberate.
ANON

*"Continue with the bending exercises,
go easy on the starches and
get yourself a nice suit with well-defined vertical stripes."*

Blueberry Tango

DEWFRESH, WILD SWEDISH BLUEBERRIES,
GENTLY FOLDED INTO NATURAL, BULGARIAN
CULTURE YOGHURT.

Mexicana Iceberg

FRESH, SHELLED GULF OF MEXICO SHRIMPS
NESTLING ON A BED OF CRISP ICEBERG LETTUCE.

Java's Sunset Surprise

THINLY SLICED, FRESH JAVANESE MANGO
IN A MERINGUE BLANKET.

A study of economics usually reveals that
the best time to buy anything is last year.
MARTY ALLEN

There is always more chance of
hitting upon something valuable when you aren't too sure
what you want to hit upon.
ALFRED NORTH WHITEHEAD

Men are not against you;
they are merely for themselves.
GENE FOWLER

I've got all the money I'll ever need if I die by 4 o'clock.
HENNY YOUNGMAN

The law of diminishing returns holds good
in almost every part of our human universe.
ALDOUS LEONARD HUXLEY

If you don't see what you want, Japan hasn't copied it yet.
STORE SIGN

The history of almost every civilization
furnishes examples of geographical expansion
coinciding with deterioration in quality.
ARNOLD J. TOYNBEE

Advice would be more acceptable
if it didn't always conflict with our plans.
ANON

People of the same trade seldom meet together
without the conversation ends in a conspiracy against the public
or in some diversion to raise prices.
ADAM SMITH

Business is a combination of war and sport.
ANDRE MAUROIS

San Julienne Salad

JULIENNE STRIPS OF RAW, SAN JOAQUIN VALLEY CARROTS.

State Street Siciliana

A SLICE OF CHICAGO-STYLE, DEEP-PAN PIZZA WITH TRADITIONAL SICILIANA TOPPING.

Coconut Caprice

FRESH, SHREDDED VIRGIN ISLANDS COCONUT MOISTENED IN ITS OWN MILK.

Sales resistance is the triumph of mind over patter.
EDMUND FULLER

Conscience is the little voice that tells you
you shouldn't have done it after you did.
ANON

Basic research
is when I'm doing what I don't know I'm doing.
WERNHER von BRAUN

Suppose you were an idiot
and suppose you were a member of Congress;
but I repeat myself.
MARK TWAIN

In Wall Street the only thing that's hard to explain is —
next week
LOUIS RUKEYSER

He has so much money that he could afford to look poor.
EDGAR WALLACE

It is not from the benevolence
of the butcher, the brewer, or the baker
that we expect our dinner,
but from their regard to their own interest.
ADAM SMITH

Reputation is a bubble which bursts
when a man tries to blow it up for himself.
EMMA CARLETON

Lack of money is the root of all evil.
GEORGE BERNARD SHAW

The voice of conscience has a difficult time
making connections with the ears.
EDGAR WATSON HOWE

Hawaii Hello!

HAWAIIAN FRUIT PUNCH –
A FRESHLY MACERATED TROPICAL
FRUIT NECTAR.

Entente Cordial

FLUFFY SOUFFLÉ OF MATURED, ENGLISH
FARMHOUSE CHEDDAR CHEESE.

Florida Compote

THINLY SLICED, CHILLED ROUNDS OF
FLORIDA ORANGE WITH A LIGHT SYRUP.

Nearly every man in the city wants a farm
until he gets it.
JACOB M. BRAUDE

Money doesn't buy friends
but it allows a better class of enemies.
LORD MANCROFT

It is taken for granted that by lunchtime
the average man has been so beaten down by life
that he will believe anything.
CHRISTOPHER MORLEY

The men who really wield, retain, and covet power
are the kind who answer bedside phones while making love.
NICHOLAS PILEGGI

Fortunes are made by buying low and selling too soon.
BARON ROTHSCHILD

Professionals built the 'Titanic' –
amateurs the Ark.
ANON

Hindsight is always twenty-twenty.
BILLY WILDER

Half the money I spend on advertising is wasted,
and the trouble is I don't know which half.
JOHN WANAMAKER

The trouble with the profit system has always been
that it was highly unprofitable to most people.
ELWYN BROOKS WHITE

I'm a self made man,
but I think if I had it to do over again,
I'd call in someone else.
ROLAND YOUNG

Louisiana Heaven

HALF A SMALL RIPE
LAFAYETTE CANTELOUPE MELON.

French Connection

CRISP SPRING CABBAGE;
TENDER YOUNG FRENCH BEANS;
KENTUCKY SPINACH; AND MANGE TOUT PEAS,
QUICKLY STIR-FRIED.

Aloha Aloha

RINGS OF JUICY HAWAIIAN PINEAPPLE —
A TASTE OF PARADISE.

There's no such thing as a free lunch.
MILTON FRIEDMAN

Money isn't everything
but it's a long way ahead of what comes next.
SIR EDWARD STOCKDALE

There's one sure way to make a businessman worry.
Tell him not to.
LEOPOLD FECHTNER

If you don't want to work,
you have to work to earn enough money so that
you won't have to work.
OGDEN NASH

I learned more about economics
from one South Dakota dust storm
than I did in all my years in college.
HUBERT HUMPHREY

It is not the crook in modern business that we fear,
but the honest man who doesn't know what he is doing.
OWEN D. YOUNG

Three things matter in a speech;
who says it, how he says it, and what he says —
and, of the three, the last matters the least.
JOHN MORLEY

Progress is a continuing effort to make the things
we eat, drink and wear as good as they used to be.
BILL VAUGHAN

It's what you learn after you know it all that counts.
JOHN WOODEN

Man is the only animal that plays poker.
DON HEROLD

"I read an article this morning that says
you can have too much fibre."

Friday Treat

MARTINI COCKTAIL WITH BEEFEATER LONDON GIN,
ITALIAN VERMOUTH AND STUFFED ITALIAN OLIVE –
GENTLY SHAKEN, NOT STIRRED (OF COURSE).

Frito Misto Maestro

FRITURE FILLET OF YOUNG NEW ENGLAND SCHROD
GARNISHED WITH CRISP WHITEBAIT MORSELS.

The Berry Thing

WHOLE, DEWFRESH, GLEN COVA RASPBERRIES.

What is clear beyond question
is that the immediate foreground is obscure.
DAILY TELEGRAPH

For every credibility gap there is a gullibility fill.
RICHARD CLOPTON

Ideas are one thing and what happens is another.
JOHN CAGE

If the facts don't fit the theory,
change the facts.
ALBERT EINSTEIN

The trouble with today's economy
is that when a man is rich, it's all on paper.
When he's broke, it's cash.
SAM MARCONI

Money is more troublesome to watch than forget.
MICHEL de MONTAIGNE

Do other men, for they would do you,
that's the true business precept.
CHARLES DICKENS

There is hardly anything in the world
that some men cannot make a little worse
and sell a little cheaper.
JOHN RUSKIN

It's what a fellow thinks he knows that hurts him.
FRANK McKINNEY HUBBARD

The best mental effort in the game of business
is concentrated on the major problem
of securing the consumer's dollar,
before the other fellow gets it.
STUART CHASE

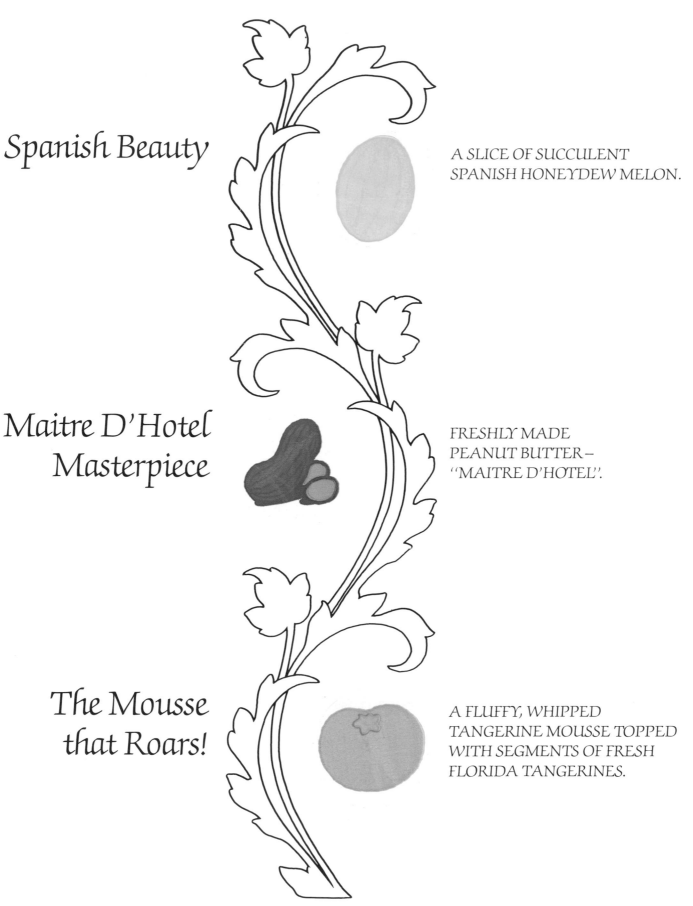

Spanish Beauty

A SLICE OF SUCCULENT
SPANISH HONEYDEW MELON.

Maitre D'Hotel
Masterpiece

FRESHLY MADE
PEANUT BUTTER—
"MAITRE D'HOTEL".

The Mousse
that Roars!

A FLUFFY, WHIPPED
TANGERINE MOUSSE TOPPED
WITH SEGMENTS OF FRESH
FLORIDA TANGERINES.

There is enough energy wasted in poker
to make a hundred thousand successful every year.
ARTHUR BRISBANE

When a fellow says, 'Well, to make a long story short,'
it's too late.
DON HERROLD

The human brain starts working the moment you are born
and never stops until you stand up to speak in public.
SIR GEORGE JESSEL

Men always try to keep women out of business
so they won't find out how much fun it really is.
VIVIEN KELLEMS

Last week is the time you should have either bought or sold,
depending on which you didn't do.
LEONARD LOUIS LEVINSON

There are two kinds of statistics,
the kind you look up and the kind you make up.
REX STOUT

Inequality of knowledge is the key to the sale.
DEIL O. GUSTAFSON

Wealth—Any income that is at least
one hundred dollars more a year than
the income of one's wife's sister's husband.
HENRY LOUIS MENCKEN

Breakages Limited,
the biggest industrial corporation in the country.
GEORGE BERNARD SHAW

If hard work is the key to success,
most people would rather pick the lock.
CLAUDE McDONALD

Deli Dill Delight

THINLY SLICED DILL, PICKLED À LA MAISON.

The Creative Crêpe

A LIGHT PANCAKE CRÊPE STUFFED WITH FRESH,
VIRGINIAN MOUNTAIN MUSHROOMS.

Pâté Frolle Frolic

A TARTLET OF FRESHLY GROUND
CALIFORNIA ALMOND PASTRY.

The best way to keep your word is not to give it.
NAPOLEON BONAPARTE

When buyers don't fall for prices,
prices must fall for buyers.
ANON

Speeches are like babies —
easy to conceive, hard to deliver.
PAT O'MALLEY

If all the rich people in the world
divided up their money amongst themselves,
there wouldn't be enough to go round.
CHRISTINA STEED

People who don't mind their own business
either have no mind or no business.
LEOPOLD FECHTNER

If one has not made a reasonable profit,
one has made a mistake.
LI XIANNIAN

Corporation. An ingenious device
for obtaining individual profit
without individual responsibility.
AMBROSE BIERCE

The speaker had a two second idea,
a two minute vocabulary and a two hour speech.
ANON

All that I know I learned after I was thirty.
GEORGE CLEMENCEAU

Work is the greatest thing in the world,
so we should always save some of it for tomorrow.
DON HEROLD

The Heavenly Hors D'Oeuvre

*SLICED CALIFORNIAN PEACH FOLDED GENTLY INTO
NEWBURYPORT GOAT'S MILK YOGHURT.*

The Epicurean Experience

*PAPER THIN SLICES OF PRIME VIRGINIA HAM,
HONEY-ROASTED AND CARVED OFF THE BONE.*

Flaky, Very Flaky

*APPLE STRUDEL –
THE TRADITIONAL BAVARIAN RECIPE.*

The quality of moral behaviour varies in inverse ratio
to the number of human beings involved.
ALDOUS LEONARD HUXLEY

If it's good, they'll stop making it.
HERBERT BLOCK

Doing business without advertising
is like winking at a girl in the dark.
You know what you're doing but no one else does.
STEWART H. BRITT

The more human beings proceed by plan,
the more effectively they may be hit by accident.
FRIEDRICH DURRENMATT

Money talks. The more money, the louder it talks.
ARNOLD ROTHSTEIN

Some persons are very decisive
when it comes to avoiding decisions.
BRENDAN FRANCIS

Nothing is sadder than having worldly standards
without worldly means.
VAN WYCK BROOKS

There are three things not worth running for –
a bus, a woman or a new economic panacea:
if you wait a bit another will come along.
DERICK HEATHCOAT AMORY

Businessmen get together
and complain about bad business
over the most expensive dinners.
ANON

When a merchant speaks of sheep he means the hide.
SWISS PROVERB

*"Another success, Robson – came in
obese, going out fat."*

The Gorgeous Grapefruit

*HALF AN ORCHARD-FRESH
FLORIDA GRAPEFRUIT*

Potato Paradiso

*FLASH-FRIED, CRISP
IDAHO POTATO SKINS
WITH A LIGHT,
SOUR CREAM DIP.*

Fragrant Fantasy

*KINGSTON BAY
JAMAICAN GINGERBREAD,
WARM FROM THE OVEN.*

He who builds a better mousetrap these days
runs into material shortages, patent-infringement suits,
works stoppages, collusive bidding, discount discrimination—
and taxes.

H. E. MARTZ

When a man needs money, he needs money,
and not a headache tablet or a prayer.

WILLIAM FEATHER

When you're down and out something always turns up—
and it's usually the noses of your friends.

ORSON WELLES

A completely planned economy
ensures that when no bacon is delivered,
no eggs are delivered at the same time.

LEO FRAIN

Research is an organized method
for keeping you reasonably dissatisfied with what you have.

CHARLES F. KETTERING

Politics is the science of how who
gets what, when and why.

SIDNEY HILLMAN

When I have an idea, I have no pencil.

ANON

Half the time when men think they are talking business,
they are wasting time.

EDGAR WATSON HOWE

A consumer is a shopper who is sore about something.

HAROLD COFFIN

I believe the twenty four hour day has come to stay.

MAX BEERBOHM

The Succulent Starter

PEELED, THOMPSON SEEDLESS GRAPES.

Sublime Stilton

SCOOPS OF THE FINEST, MATURED BLUE CHEESE
FROM MELTON MOWBRAY, ENGLAND.

Pear Fresco

LAYERED SLICES OF CONFERENCE PEAR,
INTERLEAVED WITH WHIPPED MERINGUE.

When I was young I used to think
that money was the most important thing in life;
now that I am old, I know it is.
OSCAR WILDE

It is well known what a middle-man is:
he is the man who bamboozles one party
and plunders the other.
BENJAMIN DISRAELI

Technology made large populations possible;
large populations now make technology indispensable.
JOSEPH WOOD KRUTCH

People will buy anything that's one to a customer.
SINCLAIR LEWIS

I do most of my work sitting down; that's where I shine.
ROBERT BENCHLEY

Solvency is entirely a matter of temperament
and not of income.
LOGAN PEARSALL SMITH

If you think education is expensive, try ignorance.
DEREK BOK

If you think you have someone eating out of your hand,
it's a good idea to count your fingers.
MARTIN BUXBAUM

When a man says money can do everything, that settles it;
he hasn't any.
EDGAR WATSON HOWE

Money is not an aphrodisiac:
the desire it may kindle in the female eye
is more for the cash than the carrier.
MARYA MANNES

Spanish Promise

FRESH, PLUMP VALENCIA SPANISH APRICOTS.

Montana Ranger

BREAST OF FREE-RANGE, CORN-FED
MONTANA CHICKEN,
LIGHTLY FRIED IN BATON ROUGE BATTER.

Jamaican Jamboree

FEATHER-LIGHT COOKIES, FRESHLY BAKED
WITH GROUND JAMAICAN GINGER.

Insurance is death on the instalment plan.
PHILIP SLATER

I wasn't affected by the crash of '29.
I went broke in '28.
GERALD F. LIEBERMAN

Everything comes to him who hustles while he waits.
THOMAS A. EDISON

A man who has money may be anxious,
depressed, frustrated and unhappy,
but one thing he's not—and that's broke.
BRENDAN FRANCIS

The cleverly expressed opposite
of any generally accepted idea
is worth a fortune to somebody.
F. SCOTT FITZGERALD

Never learn to do anything. If you don't learn
you'll always find someone else to do it for you.
MARK TWAIN'S MOTHER

Business is other people's money.
DELPHINE de GIRARDIN

If automation keeps up, man will atrophy all his limbs
but the push-button finger.
FRANK LLOYD WRIGHT

When ordering lunch,
the big executives are just as indecisive
as the rest of us.
WILLIAM FEATHER

True, you can't take it with you,
but then that's not the place where
it comes in so handy.
BRENDAN FRANCIS

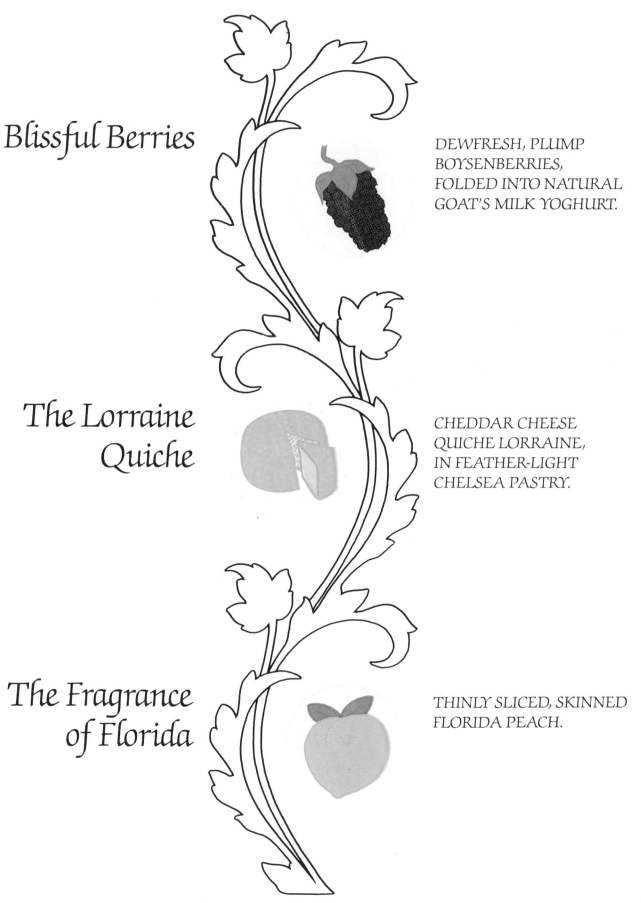

Blissful Berries

DEWFRESH, PLUMP
BOYSENBERRIES,
FOLDED INTO NATURAL
GOAT'S MILK YOGHURT.

The Lorraine Quiche

CHEDDAR CHEESE
QUICHE LORRAINE,
IN FEATHER-LIGHT
CHELSEA PASTRY.

The Fragrance of Florida

THINLY SLICED, SKINNED
FLORIDA PEACH.

Respectability: The offspring of a liaison
between a bald head and a bank accountant.
AMBROSE BIERCE

The stock market has spoiled more appetitites
than bad cooking.
WILL ROGERS

The half baked ideas of people
are better than the ideas of half baked people.
PROFESSOR WILLIAM B. SHOCKLEY

A rich man is one who isn't afraid to ask the salesman
to show him something cheaper.
LADIES HOME JOURNAL

In the ad. biz, sincerity is a commodity
bought and paid for like everything else.
MALCOLM MUGGERIDGE

"And which particular water do
you identify yourself with?"

It's called political economy
because it has nothing to do with either politics
or economy.
STEPHEN LEACOCK

A sign of celebrity is often that his name
is worth more than his services.
DANIEL J. BOORSTIN

Politicians are the same all over.
They promise to build a bridge even where there is no river.
NIKITA KHRUSHCHEV

The outlook for the businessman is usually brighter
than the outlook of the businessman.
ANON

Money is the poor people's credit card.
MARSHALL McLUHAN

The Ambrosial Apple

ONE CRISPLY DELICATE ENGLISH
COX'S ORANGE PIPPIN APPLE SALAD.

Onions à la Grecque

BUTTON ONIONS WITH CHABLIS WINE,
CONCASSE TOMATOES, OLIVE OIL,
A TOUCH OF FENNEL AND A SUGGESTION
OF CORIANDER.

Lake Lucerne Jubilation

MOIST CHERRY GATEAU TOPPED WITH FRESH
IMPORTED SWISS BLACK CHERRIES.

The gambling known as business
looks with austere disfavour upon the business
known as gambling.
AMBROSE BIERCE

I sometimes think that strategy is nothing but tactics
talked through a brass hat.
R. V. JONES

Blessed are they who have nothing to say,
and who cannot be persuaded to say it.
JAMES RUSSELL LOWELL

Budget: A mathematical confirmation of your suspicions.
JOHN A. LINCOLN

The trouble with some self-made men is that they insist
on giving everybody the recipe.
MAURICE SEITTER

It is hard to believe that a man is telling the truth
when you know that you would lie
if you were in his place.
HENRY LOUIS MENCKEN

Statistician—
A man who can go directly from an unwarranted assumption
to a preconceived conclusion.
C. KENT WRIGHT

The optimist invented the aeroplane,
the pessimist the parachute.
ANON

No man deeply engaged in serious work has time to learn.
JOSEPH HERGESHEIMER

What is research but a blind date with knowledge?
WILL HENRY

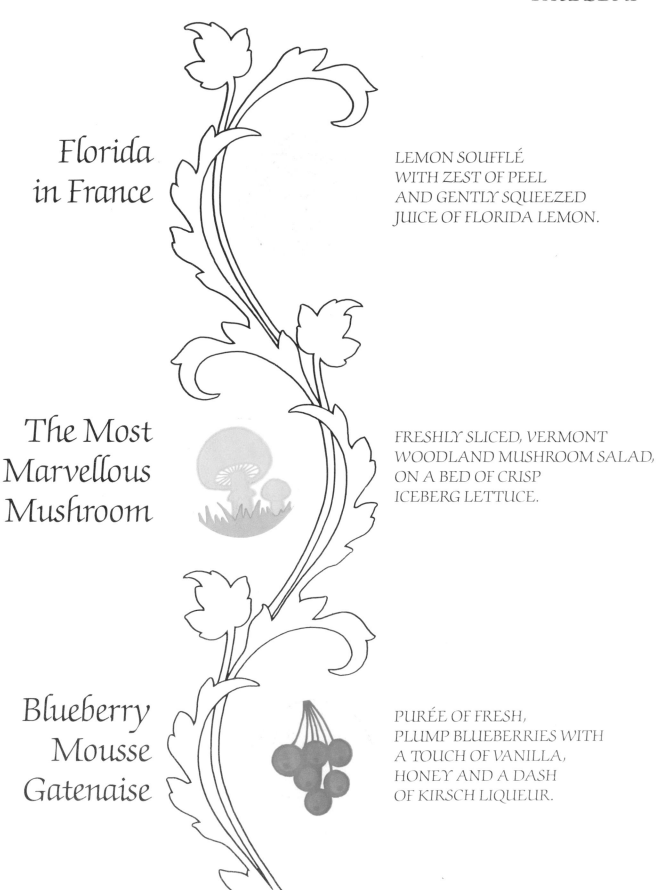

Florida
in France

LEMON SOUFFLÉ
WITH ZEST OF PEEL
AND GENTLY SQUEEZED
JUICE OF FLORIDA LEMON.

The Most
Marvellous
Mushroom

FRESHLY SLICED, VERMONT
WOODLAND MUSHROOM SALAD,
ON A BED OF CRISP
ICEBERG LETTUCE.

Blueberry
Mousse
Gatenaise

PURÉE OF FRESH,
PLUMP BLUEBERRIES WITH
A TOUCH OF VANILLA,
HONEY AND A DASH
OF KIRSCH LIQUEUR.

Nothing astonishes men so much
as common sense and plain dealing.
RALPH WALDO EMERSON

Auditors are the people who go in after the war is lost
and bayonet the wounded.
P. RUBIN

The only man who can change his mind
is the man who's got one.
EDWARD NOYES WESTCOTT

Nothing links man to man like the frequent passage
from hand to hand of cash.
WALTER SICKERT

I hate people who are wise during the event.
KENNETH TYNAN

A speech is like a love affair. Any fool can start it,
but to end it requires considerable skill.
LORD MANCROFT

People think of the inventor as a screwball,
but no one asks the inventor what he thinks of other people.
CHARLES F. KETTERING

When a person tells you,
'I'll think it over and let you know' – you know.
OLIN MILLER

Knowledge is not knowledge
until someone else knows that one knows.
LUCILIUS

You can analyse a glass of water
and you're left with a lot of chemical components
but nothing you can drink.
J. B. S. HALDANE

The Perfumed Plum

FRESH, JUICY SAN JOAQUIN VALLEY
CALIFORNIA PLUMS.

A Fantasy of Fillets

AN ASSORTMENT OF SMALL FILLETS OF
NEW ENGLAND SEA FISH,
LIGHTLY FRIED IN CAPE COD RECIPE BATTER.

Tarte aux Poires

THINLY SLICED, GLAZED PEAR,
ON A CRISP FRENCH PASTRY BASE.

The stock market has called nine
of the last five recessions.
PAUL A. SAMUELSON

I got what no millionaire's got,
I got no money.
GERALD F. LIEBERMAN

Work expands to fill the time available for its completion.
C. NORTHCOTE PARKINSON

Life is short and so is money.
BERTOLT BRECHT

Hindsight is good, foresight is better;
but second sight is best of all.
EVAN ESAR

There is nobody so irritating
as somebody with less intelligence and more sense
than we have.
DON HEROLD

Any survey of what businessmen are reading
runs smack into the open secret
that most businessmen aren't.
MARILYN BENDER

Half the world
is composed of people who have something to say and can't,
and the other half who have nothing to say
and keep on saying it.
ROBERT FROST

An ounce of emotion is equal to a ton of facts.
JOHN JUNOR

A bull does not enjoy fame in two herds.
RHODESIAN PROVERB

Sun-Tanned
and Soft

THINLY SLICED
CALIFORNIAN PEACH.

Mamma-Mia!

NEOPOLITAN PIZZA ON HOT,
STONEGROUND,
WHOLEWHEAT BASE.

The Delectable
Dessert

SLICE OF MOIST MINCE PIE
À LA MAISON.

Statistics indicate that, as a result of overwork,
modern executives are dropping like flies
on the nation's golf courses.
IRA WALLACH

One of the rarest phenomena
is a really pessimistic businessman.
MIRIAN BEARD

Bankruptcy is a legal proceeding
in which you put your money in your pants pocket
and give your coat to your creditors.
JOEY ADAMS

Be good and you will be lonesome.
MARK TWAIN

Speeches cannot be made long enough for the speakers,
nor short enough for the hearers.
JAMES PERRY

An optimist is always broke.
FRANK McKINNEY HUBBARD

Don't let your mouth write no cheque your tail can't cash.
BO DIDDLEY

I always wanted to get into politics,
but I was never light enough to make the team.
ART BUCHWALD

Don't gamble:
buy some good stock, hold it till it goes up
and then sell it—
if it doesn't go up, don't buy it!
WILL ROGERS

A corporation cannot blush.
HOWELL WALSH

"I assure you we use only French additives."

From the Vine—To You—With Love

FRESHLY-PICKED CALIFORNIAN GRAPES.

Alicante Ambrosia

THINLY SLICED, ALICANTE TOMATO SALAD
WITH A LIGHT OLIVE OIL
AND WINE VINEGAR DRESSING.

New Hampshire Pumpkin Mousse

A LIGHT CONFECTION IN A SHELL CASE OF
FEATHER-LIGHT PUFF PASTRY.

There's no such thing as 'zero risk'.
WILLIAM DRIVER

A budget is the way to go broke methodically.
ANON

The two leading recipes for success
are building a better mousetrap
and finding a bigger loophole.
EDGAR A. SHOAFF

Some problems are so complex
that it takes high intelligence
just to be undecided about them.
LAURENCE J. PETER

His quest for something new each month
leads to widespread corporate premature ejaculation.
ROBERT TOWNSEND

A good ad. should be like a good sermon;
it must not only comfort the afflicted,
it also must afflict the comfortable.
BERNICE FITZ-GIBBON

Research is something that tells you
that a jackass has two ears.
ALBERT D. LASKER

There are some people that if they don't know,
you can't tell 'em.
LOUIS ARMSTRONG

A large reputation often depends on
a small geographical sphere of influence.
ANON

Whatever you have, you must either use or lose.
HENRY FORD

The Heavenly Honeydew

SLICE OF RIPE, REFRESHING HONEYDEW MELON.

The Quintessential Quiche

FEATHER-LIGHT AND BURSTING WITH HOME-CURED
KENTUCKY HAM.

The Dark Swiss Secret

PROFITEROLES -
NUGGETS OF LIGHT CHOUX PASTRY,
SMOTHERED WITH DARK SWISS CHOCOLATE SAUCE.

There is a way to make a lot of money in the market;
unfortunately it is the same way
to lose a lot of money in the market.
PETER PASSELL + LEONARD ROSE

If you hear that 'everybody' is buying a certain stock,
ask who is selling.
JAMES DINES

After learning the tricks of the trade,
many of us think we know the trade.
WILLIAM FEATHER

To make a speech immortal
you don't have to make it everlasting.
LESLIE HORE-BELISHA

Technology – the knack of so arranging the world
that we don't have to experience it.
MAX FRISCH

Thomas Edison did not invent the first talking machine.
He invented the first one you could turn off.
HERBERT V. PROCHNOW

Nothing's so apt to undermine your confidence in a product
as knowing that the commercial selling it
has been approved by the company that makes it.
FRANKLIN P. JONES

What after all is a halo?
It's only one more thing to keep clean.
CHRISTOPHER FRY

I backed the right horse,
and then the wrong horse went and won.
HENRY HERMAN

I'll give you a definite maybe.
SAMUEL GOLDWYN

Juicy Florida Goodness

SEGMENTS OF OSCEOLA COUNTY FLORIDA GRAPEFRUIT.

Stockholm Succulence

PAPER-THIN SLICES OF FIRM GEORGIAN CUCUMBER, MARINADED IN A LIGHT, SWEDISH VINAIGRETTE DRESSING.

The Kettleman Hills Secret

KETTLEMEN HILLS, CALIFORNIA RECIPE, MOIST AND MARVELLOUS FRUIT CAKE.

If necessity is the mother of invention,
what was papa doing?
RUTH WEEKLEY

Some people can stay longer in an hour
than others can in a week
WILLIAM DEAN HOWELLS

I feel when people say 'bigger and better'
they should say 'bigger and badder.'
MARIE ELIZABETH KANE

Advertising may be described as
the science of arresting the human intelligence
long enough to get money from it.
STEPHEN LEACOCK

Keep in mind the fact that Ralph Nader
could be the first customer for your new product.
ANON

What a man knows at 50 which he didn't know at 20
is, for the most part, incommunicable.
ADLAI STEVENSON

The decision is maybe and that's final.
GRAFFITI

Wall Street is where prophets tell us what will happen
and profits tell us what did happen.
ROBERT ORBEN

A businessman
is one who talks golf all morning at the office
and business all afternoon on the course.
ANON

The recipe for a good speech includes some shortening.
ANON

Copacabana Temptation

NATURAL YOGHURT, FLAVOURED WITH
SMALL CUBES AND THE JUICE OF
BRAZILIAN MANGO.

Grenouilles Provençale

IMPORTED, FRENCH FROGS LEGS,
WITH CRUSHED PROVENÇALE GARLIC CLOVES.

Parisian Walnut Gateau

A MOIST DELICACY FLAVOURED AND TOPPED WITH
FINELY CHOPPED WALNUTS.

The Ultimate Executive Lunch Book

Special thanks to Donald "The Guru" Keith

Published by
Hurley Style Limited
The Manor House
Hurley
Berkshire SL6 5NB
England

Hurley Style Limited
Heritage Drive
Portsmouth
New Hampshire
03801 USA

Copyright © 1986 Stefan White

The book was designed and produced by
W Foulsham & Co. Ltd
Yeovil Road,
Slough SL1 4JH
England

ISBN 0-572-01410-4

Cartoons reproduced by permission of Punch

Made in England

ABOUT THE AUTHOR

Professor Tymus Munney is the pen-name of a mildly eccentric Englishman, Stefan White. His only previous book was under the pen-names of Pettigrew and Blenkinsopp and was entitled 'An Introduction to the Principles of Aeronautical Design and the Science of Aerodynamics'. Produced in a similarly prestigious fashion it contains the Executive Paper Aeroplane Making Kit. With detailed tear-out sheets and full construction details, the executive can make eight different, sophisticated paper aeroplanes to fly in the privacy of the office.

Whilst awaiting inspiration for his next book he is working on an exciting new project to cross a chicken with a banjo. The interbreeding and genetics are proving a problem but he hopes to achieve the desired result which is, of course, a chicken that plucks itself.

ABOUT THE QUOTATIONS

Your daily ration of ten thought-provoking quotations has been extracted from a new book entitled 'The Great Business Quotations'. This is published by Lyle Stuart Inc. and launched in September 1986. Edited by Rolf White, there are 3000 quotations, covering 80 different aspects of business life from sources as varied as President Reagan, Joseph Stalin, Al Capone and Bob Hope. The book is full of humorous common sense comments, worth repeating in speeches or just to impress your colleagues with your erudite wit and wisdom. The compilation took 3 years to complete and permission to extract from this entertaining and educational work is gratefully acknowledged. 'The Great Business Quotations' is available from all major bookstores at $15.00.